Contents

The Powers

of the President

 When the tall, elegant man named George Washington took the oath as the first president of the United States, no one knew exactly what the new president would do. At first, no one even knew what to call him. "His Elective Majesty" was one suggestion and "His Highness, the President of the United States and Protector of the Rights of the Same" was another. Finally, the House of Representatives decided that a simple title would be best: "president of the United States."

Washington knew more than anyone that each of his actions as president was very important. He thought carefully about how to make sure that the office of president was treated with dignity. He drove in a gilded carriage and held formal parties.

Opposite:
George Washington first established many of the roles and traditions now associated with the presidency.

When President Washington visited Massachusetts, the governor, John Hancock, invited Washington to visit him. Washington replied politely that instead the governor, if he wished, could visit the president. Washington made it very clear that the office of president was the highest in the land, deserving the greatest respect and honor.

Since Washington took the oath of office, promising to "preserve, protect and defend the Constitution of the United States," 39 other presidents have taken the same oath. Presidents today do not drive in gilded carriages, and they are more likely to pose for photographs than greet visitors at the kind of formal reception hosted by George and Martha Washington. A great deal has changed about the office and duties of the president since George Washington's time, but this much stays the same: The office of president is still the most powerful and most important position in the United States.

Creating the Office of President

After the colonists won their independence from Great Britain, they were governed by Congress under a colonial agreement called the Articles of Confederation. Congress had some powers under the Articles, such as the power to declare war. As a whole, however, the government was weak and undefined. Foreign powers did not expect the new United States to survive very long.

In 1787, delegates from the states met at the Philadelphia Statehouse and decided to write a new constitution. The delegates worked out many difficult problems in setting up a new form of government for the United States. They decided to create a balanced government, dividing power among three main branches: the Congress, or legislative branch; the judicial branch; and the executive branch. The head of the executive branch would be the head of the government.

Up to that point, the delegates were very clear about the kind of government they wanted to create. The role of the chief executive, however, raised many questions.

The Constitutional Convention of 1787 created the system of government we use today.

7

In 1789, George Washington was inaugurated as America's first president at a ceremony in New York.

To prevent the president from ever becoming too powerful, the Founders, as we call the delegates to the Constitutional Convention, made sure that the other branches of government could check, or control, the actions of the president. For example, the president has the power to work out treaties with other nations, but the Senate must approve a treaty before it can go into effect.

The most dramatic way that Congress can check the president is through impeachment. Congress can bring to trial a president suspected of serious wrongdoing. Only one president was formally impeached. The House of Representatives impeached Andrew Johnson (served 1865–1869) in 1868, but he was acquitted in his trial before the Senate.

The delegates worked out answers to many other questions about the chief executive. How many people should hold the office? Some of the delegates thought that a council of three should divide the power of the chief executive. Finally, however, a majority of the delegates agreed that one person could best carry out the duties of the president of the United States.

Another question to be decided was the length of the president's term in office. Some of the delegates suggested that the president should serve a long term, from 15 to 20 years, with no chance for re-election. In that way, the president would not have to think about whether his actions were popular with the voters. Other delegates thought that the president should serve only a few years. Finally the delegates agreed on a four-year term of office. They did not set a limit to how many terms a president could serve. Franklin Roosevelt (FDR) (served 1933–1945) was re-elected three times. The Twenty-Second Amendment, which went into effect in 1951, limited all future presidents to two full terms.

One of the most important questions the delegates had to answer was, What should the president do? What powers would the president have? The Founders listed some specific duties of the president and some of the specific powers given to him. However, during the two centuries since the Constitution was written, the powers and responsibilities

Andrew Johnson is the only president to ever be impeached.

of the president have grown. Congress has passed laws that give the president certain powers. And through custom and tradition the president has also acquired additional duties and assumed other powers.

The Roles of the President

The Constitution mentions five jobs that the president must perform. Juggling these varied roles is not always easy. In addition, over the years the president has acquired two more roles that are not found in the Constitution.

First of all, the president is the head of state of the United States. That means that the president symbolizes all the American people. As head of state, the president acts as host to monarchs and heads of other governments visiting the United States. The president entertains the leaders of other nations at state dinners and entertainments. The president also gives out awards and medals, and meets entertainers, astronauts, and athletes. In some countries, such as Great Britain, the person who acts as head of state is not the same person who directs the government.

As chief diplomat, the president is responsible for the treaties and agreements that make up the nation's foreign policy. Foreign policy is the way the nation relates to the rest of the world. The president can choose to formally recognize the existence of a new nation, for example. In late 1991, President

The Three Branches of Government

EXECUTIVE

The President

- Symbol of our nation and head of state
- Shapes and conducts foreign policy and acts as chief diplomat
- Chief administrator of the federal government
- Commander-in-chief of armed forces
- Authority to pass or veto congressional bills, plans, and programs
- Appoints and removes non-elected officials
- Leader of political party

LEGISLATIVE

The Congress
The Senate
The House of Representatives

- Chief lawmaking body
- Conducts investigations into matters of national importance
- Has power to impeach or remove any civil officer from office, including the president
- Can amend the Constitution
- The Senate is made up of 100 senators—2 from each state
- The House of Representatives is made up of 435 congressional representatives, apportioned to each state according to population

JUDICIAL

The Supreme Court

- Protects the Constitution
- Enforces commands of the executive and legislative branches
- Protects the rights of individuals and shields citizens from unfair laws
- Can declare laws unconstitutional
- Defines the laws of our nation

George Bush recognized the independence of the Baltic republics of Estonia, Latvia, and Lithuania, as well as Russia, all of which were part of what once was called the Soviet Union. Although the Senate must confirm all treaties, the president sets the tone for our dealings with the rest of the world.

The Constitution says that "the executive Power shall be vested in a President of the United States of America." Therefore, the president is the chief executive and the chief administrator of the national

As commander-in-chief of the armed forces, the president must make decisions critical to national security. Here, President Bush meets with his advisors during the Persian Gulf War.

government. In fact, the president is actually the boss of more than three million employees of the federal government. Such employees range from letter carriers to customs officials, from clerks to department heads. Of course, the president does not personally supervise all the departments and agencies, but is ultimately responsible for their smooth operation.

One of the most visible roles of the president is as commander-in-chief of the armed forces. The president must have the approval of Congress to declare war. However, the president can authorize the use of troops overseas without declaring war. In fact, United States troops fought for many years in

Korea (1950–1953) and in Vietnam (1957–1975) without a formal declaration of war.

In 1973, Congress acted to check the power of the president to commit United States forces to combat. Now the president can order troops into battle without the approval of Congress only if the combat is expected to last less than 60 days.

All members of the United States armed forces answer to the president. In 1951, at the height of the Korean War, President Harry Truman (served 1945–1953) removed the popular general Douglas MacArthur from his command. MacArthur had publicly criticized Truman's decisions about how the war should be fought, ignoring the fact that Truman was his commander.

As commander-in-chief, the president must authorize and oversee the actions of any military operation. In 1794, President George Washington called on federal troops to go into Pennsylvania to put down an uprising called the Whiskey Rebellion. Today, modern communications allow presidents to supervise any scene of combat almost as closely as the generals in the field. Some presidents have chosen to let the military make their own decisions, and others have become closely involved. President Richard Nixon (served 1969–1974), for example, made many key military decisions as commander-in-chief during the Vietnam War.

One of the most grim responsibilities of the president is to choose whether to authorize the use

President Richard Nixon made many key military decisions during the Vietnam War. In many ways, this was the first war run from the White House.

14

of nuclear weapons. In order to end the war with Japan, President Truman made the decision to drop atomic bombs on Japan during the closing days of World War II (1939–1945). Today, wherever the president goes, a small black box goes, too. In order to launch missiles armed with nuclear weapons, the president must use this black box to send electronic signals to a military base. Of course, the president can also work to reduce the number of nuclear weapons in the world through mutual agreements and treaties with the heads of other nations.

In 1991, President Bush announced a plan to greatly reduce America's nuclear weapons across the world. A few weeks later, Mikhail Gorbachev, president of the now disbanded Soviet Union, responded with a similar plan. If carried out, these plans would soon eliminate thousands of nuclear weapons worldwide. Since then, with the breakup of the Soviet Union, control of the nuclear weapons has passed on to Russia, which is headed by Boris Yeltsin, and to the different leaders of the other independent states.

Even with all the powers of the executive office, the president cannot make new laws. It is only Congress, the legislative branch, that can do that. However, the president does have some control over the bills that the Congress considers. The president can propose bills and make suggestions to Congress. Each year the president first presents a program of desired new laws in the State of the Union address, a formal speech delivered to both houses of Congress. Then, throughout the year, the president sends detailed proposals for new laws, which the executive staff has developed under the president's direction.

The success of a president's proposals depends in part on how many members of Congress are from the same political party as the president. If the president's party has a majority in Congress, the president has an easier time getting proposals through the legislature.

The State of the Union speech outlines a president's desired laws and programs for the coming year. Here, Lyndon Johnson addresses the Congress.

The president, as holder of the nation's highest office, is also the head of a political party. The president works with the leaders of the party to plan the party's future. He endorses and campaigns for party members and helps to raise funds for the party as well as members running for office.

The president and vice-president are the only officials in the government who are elected by the entire nation. The president is expected to work on behalf of each American, and to put the interests of the American public before all others.

Finally, the president is the chief citizen of the United States. And the president's family is the chief family. The First Family, as the president's family is commonly called, is an object of endless curiosity to Americans and to the rest of the world. The media—newspapers, television, radio, magazines—constantly report on the First Family's beliefs, values, style, and habits.

Who Can Become President?

The Founders set down in the Constitution very few specific rules about who can become president. They stated that the president must be a "natural born Citizen," meaning a U.S. citizen from birth. The president must also be at least 35 years old and must have lived in the United States for no less than 14 years.

In order to actually be elected, however, a few other characteristics are traditionally required. To even become a serious candidate for president, a person needs years of experience and many contacts in politics. Most presidential candidates have previously served terms as governors, senators, or members of the House of Representatives. A few have been prominent military figures or members of a president's Cabinet. (The Cabinet is the group of the president's closest and most influential advisors.) Almost all have been college graduates and have worked at a profession before being appointed to political office.

It is unlikely that any candidate without some personal wealth and wealthy friends and supporters could run a successful national campaign. Running for president costs millions of dollars. Congress passed a law in 1988 limiting the spending on a presidential campaign to about $89 million. A candidate cannot pay it all alone, but a strong contender has good contacts that will help raise the money.

All presidents so far have been white and male. However, in 1984, Geraldine Ferraro ran for vice-president as part of Walter Mondale's presidential campaign. In 1988, Jesse Jackson, an African American, ran strongly in the early days of the presidential campaign. All presidents but one, Roman Catholic John Kennedy (served 1961–1963), have been Protestant. Most experts feel sure that as more women and members of minority groups run for elective office, there will be more female and minority candidates running for president.

Jesse Jackson's presidential campaign in 1988 opened the door for other African American candidates in the future.

Jacqueline and John Kennedy

The wife of the president has a most unusual job. She is not elected to any office, she receives no salary, she has no official powers. Yet no one would deny that the First Lady, as she is called, wields considerable power.

Some presidents' wives have been criticized for having too much influence on their husbands' administrations. Rosalyn Carter, who sometimes attended Cabinet meetings, made no effort to deny the influence she had on Jimmy Carter (served 1977–1981). "I have an awesome responsibility and many opportuni-

ties as First Lady," she once said. "The president of the United States cares what I think. I find myself in the eye of history. I have influence, and I know it."

Other First Ladies have been even more involved in government. Eleanor Roosevelt went on information-gathering trips for her husband, Franklin, who was crippled by polio. She considered herself his eyes and ears. When President Woodrow Wilson (served 1913–1921) became ill in 1919, he was unable to meet with anyone for eight months. Edith Wilson became the president's messenger and personal advisor. Because she had so much influence, many said that she was running the country.

Many First Ladies have dedicated themselves to work that benefits the nation. Jacqueline Kennedy restored the public rooms of the White House. She asked for—and received—the support of the American people to make the "people's house" beautiful. Lady Bird Johnson worked tirelessly on projects to beautify the nation's highways, by planting native wildflowers and bushes that do not need much pruning and tending.

Dolley Madison

Perhaps one of the best-known and most remarkable First Ladies was one of the first, Dolley Madison. Known for her gaiety and

Eleanor Roosevelt

hospitality, Mrs. Madison is also known for risking capture by the British to save a famous portrait of George Washington painted by Gilbert Stuart. Just before the British burned that building during the War of 1812, Dolley Madison fled from the White House. Unable to wait for the portrait to be unscrewed from the wall, Dolley ordered that the glass be broken and the picture cut from the frame.

Presidents Who Have

Changed the Office

When President Theodore ("Teddy") Roosevelt (served 1901–1909) left the White House in 1909, William Howard Taft (served 1909–1913) took his place. Roosevelt and Taft were men of the same generation and the same political party. Roosevelt had personally selected Taft as his party's next presidential candidate. But Roosevelt was surprised by the way Taft behaved as the president. In fact, the two men could not have differed more in how they viewed the power of the office.

Enthusiastic and active, Teddy Roosevelt said that the president should be "a steward of the people." He declared that the president of the nation must "do all he could for the people and

Opposite:
Franklin Delano Roosevelt was in office longer than any other president in history. He served for 12 years.

21

not . . . content himself with . . . keeping his talents undamaged in a napkin."

Taft, on the other hand, said that the president should use no power that could not be traced very clearly to the Constitution or to a particular law passed by Congress.

When the many delegates to the Constitutional Convention had finished all their debates and their arguments about the presidency, they left the actual powers of the president quite vague. Although the Constitution gives some specific powers to the president, it also says that the president has what is known as "executive power." The debate about exactly what "executive power" means has never been completely agreed upon, as shown by Roosevelt's "open" view and Taft's "closed" view.

Wartime Presidents and Additional Powers

Whenever the United States has gone to war, the president has faced numerous hard decisions. The armed forces require many things, starting with soldiers and including supplies, transportation, and housing. The military and the nation must be kept safe from spies and traitors. The nation's economy must be kept in control, while factories produce the weapons, ammunition, uniforms, boots, and other things needed by the soldiers. Wartime presidents have usually asked for additional powers to accomplish the overwhelming tasks of running the armed forces and the nation. In some cases, critics have felt that a few wartime presidents have assumed far too much power.

The Civil War (1861–1865) began almost as soon as Abraham Lincoln became president. It was a war between Northern States (called the Union) and Southern States (called the Confederacy) over differing views of how the country should be run. This included the practice of slavery as well as other issues. The nation was at peace for only 48 days while Lincoln was in office.

During the Civil War Lincoln (served 1861–1865) placed the state of Maryland under military rule. He did this to be sure that Maryland did not join the Confederacy. He even suspended the writ of *habeas corpus*, which meant that people who had been arrested for sympathizing with the South could not demand to appear before a judge to learn why they were being held. The writ of *habeas corpus* prevents people from being arrested without evidence against them. The Supreme Court decided that only Congress could suspend the writ of *habeas corpus*, but Lincoln ignored this decision. In the other border states, President Lincoln took similar steps as he felt they were needed.

The nation was at war for all but 48 days that Abraham Lincoln served as president.

23

Congress gave Woodrow Wilson great powers during World War I.

Of course, President Lincoln's bold actions were criticized. Lincoln calmly said, however, that he would do whatever was necessary to preserve the Union and the Constitution.

During World War I, President Woodrow Wilson faced many of the same problems that Abraham Lincoln had faced. The war began in Europe in 1914, and at first the United States tried to stay out of it. In 1916, Germany announced that its submarines would attack any ships found within a war zone around Great Britain. In 1917, Wilson asked Congress to pass a bill authorizing the arming of United States merchant ships to protect them against attack. The bill did not pass. Wilson ordered the arming of the merchant fleet anyway.

Once the United States entered the war, in 1917, Congress gave Wilson great powers. He was in charge of getting an army ready for war in Europe and for supplying the army with what it needed. It was a huge job, and soon departments and agencies of the executive branch were involved in almost every part of American life.

The executive branch was authorized to supervise the draft, under which nearly 10 million men were listed for possible service in the armed forces. Once the army was stationed in Europe, providing it with supplies and equipment was hard. Toward the end of the war, the government simply took control of poorly run businesses that were vital parts of the war effort, including the railroads, the telephone company, and the telegraph and cable companies. A specially created War Industries Board told businesses what to make and how much they could charge the government for goods that the government purchased from them.

The government Food Administration rationed sugar and other items. It also urged all Americans to save food and to plant vegetable gardens. The Committee on Public Information used writers, artists, and lecturers to create support among the people for the war effort.

When the war was finally won, the Senate showed President Wilson that it had powers, too. Wilson had worked hard on the treaty to end the war. He was proud that the treaty set up a League of Nations, a group in which nations could discuss their problems. However, the Senate refused to approve the treaty.

Years later, in 1973, Congress once again cut back the powers of the president after a war. At that time, the nation was haunted by the Vietnam War, a war that Congress had never declared. Over President Nixon's veto, Congress passed a bill (War Powers Act) that limited the president's powers to send American troops into combat. Today, some people feel that parts of the act are unconstitutional. However, when President Bush sent troops to the Persian Gulf in 1991, he was careful to obtain the approval of Congress for his actions.

Other Presidents Who Made Their Mark

Some of the most dramatic changes in the power of the president have occurred during wartime. But many changes have occurred in peacetimes.

Thomas Jefferson (served 1801–1809) was an advocate of a "strict construction" of the Constitution. He believed the president had only those powers specifically granted by the Constitution. However, later events convinced Jefferson to change his mind.

In 1803, Emperor Napoleon of France (1769–1821) made an amazing offer to two

As president, Thomas Jefferson approved the Louisiana Purchase, which greatly increased the size of our nation.

American diplomats, Robert Livingston, minister to France, and James Monroe, a powerful minister-at-large (and future president). He offered to sell them all of the Louisiana Territory, the vast French lands west of the Mississippi River. The American diplomats had no authority from Congress or from President Jefferson to accept such an offer. Nor could they commit the nation to paying for the purchase. It would take months to get instructions from across the sea. The diplomats had no idea what to do. What if they accepted the offer and then Congress refused to pay Napoleon? However, the two men decided the offer was too good to pass up. They decided to offer $15 million in a treaty for the territory, and Napoleon accepted.

Now President Jefferson had to decide what to do. Despite the fact that the Constitution does not mention buying land, Jefferson decided to ask Congress to approve the treaty outlining the terms of the purchase. After a long debate, the Senate finally approved the treaty. When the House of Representatives passed a bill authorizing the money to pay Napoleon, Jefferson signed the treaty. His actions doubled the size of the United States.

Teddy Roosevelt was another president who greatly increased the land that was controlled by the government of the United States. However, President Roosevelt did not buy any new territory.

Roosevelt, who loved outdoor life, persuaded Congress to give the president control over public

lands that could be set aside as national forests. Roosevelt feared that lumber companies and other developers would leave little wilderness for the people to enjoy. Previous presidents had created national forests of more than 50 million acres; Roosevelt set aside more than 190 million acres of forested land.

One president above all changed the way the national government operates. That was President Franklin Delano Roosevelt. When Roosevelt became president in 1933, the nation was suffering in the Great Depression. Public panic caused the stock market to lose millions in 1929, causing the entire economy to collapse. Factories and stores went out of business because people had no money to buy products. By the end of 1932, there were 12 million Americans without jobs. Most frightening of all, banks began to close their doors. People lost all the money they had in their bank accounts. They lost their farms and their homes. Many Americans were starving.

Roosevelt responded to the crisis with great energy. He asked Congress for extraordinary powers and Congress quickly gave those powers to him. First, the president took charge of the nation's banks and the nation's money. He decided that the government must borrow large amounts of money from the banks and spend it to get the economy working again.

Roosevelt—with the approval of Congress—set up new agencies, administrations, and commissions to deal with the problems of the nation. Some agencies gave direct relief to the poor and homeless. Others regulated business and the economy. Still others created jobs.

As a result of Roosevelt's programs, the federal government was changed forever. The national government had taken on the job of looking after the welfare of the American people. The national government became *the* government as far as most Americans were concerned. The state and local governments were no longer as important.

The size of the government, the number of agencies, the number of people employed by the government, all grew tremendously under FDR. When Roosevelt died in 1945, the United States government employed more than 3 million people. Only 650,000 had been government employees before Roosevelt took office.

Opposite: Theodore "Teddy" Roosevelt was known as a "trust-buster" who broke up the unfair power of many big businesses. He was often shown "carrying a big stick," which was a symbol of his power.

Richard Nixon resigned from office on August 9, 1974.

Richard Nixon was re-elected for a second term as president in 1972 with the largest popular majority of any president in history. Yet on August 9, 1974, he became the only president to resign from office. Nixon resigned because he was about to be impeached on charges of obstructing justice, abusing his power, and refusing to honor orders from Congress to surrender White House tapes of key conversations in which he gave illegal orders.

The charges against Nixon all started with a scandal known as Watergate. During the 1972 election, five men broke into the Democratic National Headquarters in Washington's Watergate hotel. The burglars were going to hide special devices in the office of the head of the Democratic National Committee. These devices, called "bugs," would allow outsiders to listen to phone calls and conversations.

The burglars, it turned out, had connections to Nixon's campaign organization and even to White House staff members. Instead of investigating the scandal, and firing those involved, Nixon ordered a "cover-up." He announced to the American people that there had been a full investigation and that no one on his staff was involved with Watergate.

Over time, investigators found evidence of Nixon's lie. They also found evidence of other crimes committed by his staff. There had been illegal contributions to Nixon's campaign fund and a series of dirty tricks played on his political opponents.

As the sad story was told, the House of Representatives gathered evidence to impeach Nixon. When Nixon resigned, vice-president Gerald Ford (served 1974–1977), took his place. One of the first acts of the new president was to use a special power of the of-

H.R. Haldeman

fice: a presidential pardon. Ford pardoned Nixon and made the ex-president immune to any further proceedings.

Congress acted quickly after Watergate to "open up" the national government and to end the wall of secrecy that separated the government from the people. It passed other measures that took back from the executive branch some of the powers that had once rested with Congress.

The Watergate affair proved that the constitutional system of checks on the power of the president still works. Congress and the judiciary had stopped Nixon's abuse of office. The unfortunate result of the Watergate scandal was the loss of the trust and confidence of many Americans in their own government.

The Watergate hotel

How the President

Works with Congress

Before accepting the invitation to run for vice-president on the team with John F. Kennedy in 1960, Lyndon Baines Johnson served in Congress, first in the House of Representatives, then in the Senate. In 1960, he was Senate majority leader, having held the most important position in the Senate for five years. Many people were surprised that Johnson accepted the usually humdrum position of vice-president, for as majority leader, he held the reins of the Senate. Then, on November 22, 1963, President Kennedy was fatally shot in Dallas, Texas. Lyndon Johnson (served 1963–1969) immediately took the oath of office as president while on board *Air Force One,* the presidential plane, as it flew back from Dallas to Washington, D.C.

Opposite:
Lyndon Johnson persuaded the Congress to follow his policies more successfully than any other president in recent history.

33

Johnson was a master at rounding up the votes he needed. Using what his peers called "the treatment," Johnson used his personal charm and power to persuade lawmakers to support his policies. Johnson's "treatment" usually involved intense heart-to-heart talks with those whose help he needed. No other president since has been as successful in getting his way. Before President Johnson's administration became bogged down in the long and unpopular Vietnam War, Congress passed hundreds of bills that were part of Johnson's plan to create a "Great Society."

The President as Chief Policymaker

At the beginning of each session of Congress, the members of both houses of Congress, the members of the Supreme Court, the members of the Cabinet, the foreign diplomatic corps, and other invited guests wait in the House of Representatives for the president to deliver the traditional State of the Union address.

The State of the Union speech is very important; with it the president recaps the year that has past and then outlines the plans for the coming year in the country.

Very soon after delivering the State of the Union address, the

president must send to Congress the proposed budget for the year. The budget outlines all the money that will be needed to run each part of the federal government.

The president also delivers an economic report to Congress every year. It outlines how the nation's businesses, banks, workers, stock markets, and consumers are doing.

The president may also send special messages to Congress about urgent topics. He may even go to Congress and deliver the message in person, if it is urgent enough. In the past, when presidents have asked Congress to declare war, they usually did so from a podium in the House of Representatives.

When a president wants Congress to make a law, he does not actually submit bills to Congress. The executive branch may prepare and write bills, but then a member of the House must submit a bill in the House; a senator must start a bill in the Senate.

Once a bill begins its journey through Congress, the president can try to move it along by keeping in touch with important congressional leaders. Usually this is done by phoning or visiting with key members of Congress to ensure their support.

Of course, the president can work in reverse. The president can try to prevent Congress from passing bills that are different from those in the executive program. When Congress passes a bill, it goes to the president for signing. If the president signs the bill, it becomes law.

The president can do one of three things with a bill submitted for signing. First, the president might simply sign it into law.

The second choice of the president for a bill is to veto it outright. That means the president refuses to sign the bill. Instead, the chief executive returns it to the house of Congress where it started. Often, the president sends along a list of objections.

If supporters of the bill can manage to get two-thirds of the lawmakers in each house of Congress to override the president's veto, the bill passes into law. Because Congress very seldom overrides a presidential veto, the president's threat to veto a bill is often enough to kill a bill or get it changed.

Third, the president might do nothing. If Congress is still in session, the bill becomes law in ten days (not counting Sundays) even without the presidential signature. The president may choose this option to show dislike of the measure when Congress would surely override (cancel by outvoting) a veto. This rarely happens.

If a bill comes to the president to sign at the end of a congressional session, the president may choose to "pocket" the bill, or do nothing. If Congress adjourns within ten days, the bill is dead, killed by the president's "pocket veto." Franklin Roosevelt used the pocket veto more than any other president; he pocketed 263 bills. President Grover Cleveland (served 1885–1889; 1893–1897) comes in second with only 100 bills pocketed.

★★★★★★ THE CHAIN OF COMMAND ★★★★★★

When a president dies in office, the vice-president becomes president. The new president then selects a vice-president, who takes office with the approval of a vote of both houses of Congress. When Richard Nixon was president, the vice-president, Spiro Agnew (served 1969–1973), resigned because he was under investigation for a number of crimes, including bribery and tax evasion. Nixon nominated Gerald Ford to replace Agnew, and Congress confirmed the nomination. Then, when Nixon resigned in 1974, Ford became president. Ford was the only man in history to become president without having been elected president or vice-president. Ford nominated Nelson Rockefeller as vice-president. Rockefeller was then confirmed by Congress in 1974.

In the unlikely event that the offices of both president and vice-president are vacant at the same time, the Speaker of the House is next in line to become president. The succession then goes to the president *pro tempore* of the Senate. (Since the vice-president of the United States is president of the Senate, the president *pro*

Gerald R. Ford

tempore acts as temporary president of the Senate in the vice-president's absence.) Succession to the presidency is then followed by the secretary of state, secretary of the Treasury, secretary of defense, attorney general, and on through each of the Cabinet offices in the order in which the departments were established. The last in line is the secretary of education.

For obvious reasons, the president and vice-president never fly on the same airplane.

Popular Votes and

Electoral Votes

 The 1976 presidential election was a
close, hard-fought race. Jimmy Carter
won 50.03 percent of the popular vote;
his opponent, Gerald Ford, lost with
47.97 percent of the popular vote. However, the
popular vote does not decide who wins the election.
The actual election was even closer than the popular
vote shows. If only a few more voters in a few key
states had voted for Ford, he would have had
enough electoral votes to become president—even
though Carter would still have had the majority of
the popular vote in most other states.

What are electoral votes, and why do we have
them? The answer goes back to the Constitutional
Convention and debates about how the president

Opposite:
John F. Kennedy
was one of the
most personally
popular presidents
in American
history.

should be elected. Most of the delegates did not think that people should vote directly for the president. Travel and communication in the 1700s were very difficult. The Founders did not think that most voters would be able to learn enough about the candidates to make good choices.

The Founders decided that a special Electoral College would actually select the president and vice-president. The Founders left most of the details of how the system would work to the states. For a number of reasons, the system as it was outlined in the Constitution worked as the Founders intended only when George Washington was elected.

This is how the Electoral College system is supposed to work. Each state has the same number of electors as it has senators and representatives in Congress. Every state has two senators, but the number of representatives depends on the state's population. For example, California has 45 representatives, and Delaware has 1. (The larger a state's population, the more representatives that state is allowed.)

The Founders thought that the state legislatures should select the electors, and that each state legislature should determine how it will select its electors. Today,

Jimmy Carter edged out Gerald Ford in the 1976 election by only a few electoral votes.

electors meet in their states to vote. Each elector casts two votes. One vote is for president, the other is for vice-president.

The electoral votes are delivered to Congress, where they are counted before the members of both houses. To become president, a candidate must receive a majority of the votes from all the electors (roughly, more than all the other candidates combined). The person with the second highest number of electoral votes, providing that total is also a majority of all the electoral votes, becomes vice-president.

If no candidate receives a majority of votes, or if there is a tie, then the House of Representatives chooses the president. Each state has one vote. If there is a tie in the votes for vice-president, or no candidate gets a majority of votes for vice-president, the Senate selects the vice-president by a vote.

What Changed the System?

When the Founders were debating and preparing the Constitution, they could not predict the important role that political parties would play in the nation. The electoral system worked well when George Washington was running for office, because there were no parties. During both times he ran for president, Washington received one vote from each of the electors.

By the third presidential election, however, political parties had become a firm fixture in

American life. Once political parties took hold, strange things started to happen in elections. In 1796, for example, the electors chose John Adams (served 1797–1801), a member of the Federalist party, as president. Thomas Jefferson, a member of the opposing party, the Democratic-Republicans, became the nation's vice-president.

In 1800, the Democratic-Republicans hoped to elect Jefferson as president and Aaron Burr as vice-president. The electors accordingly cast one vote for each man. There was a tie; the election had to be decided in the House, and Burr almost became president instead of Jefferson.

To avoid a similar problem, in following elections, the Twelfth Amendment was added to the Constitution in 1804. It stated that the electors should vote separately for the president and the vice-president.

During the 1800s, other important changes occurred in the way Americans selected their president. Many more people were allowed to vote. In the early days of the nation, only people with property could vote. Gradually, states relaxed their rules so that most white males could vote. Eventually, further amendments to the Constitution gave the right to vote to African Americans and women. Another amendment eliminated the poll tax (a fee for voting), allowing the poor to vote. And after the election of Thomas Jefferson, the voters took over the job of selecting their state's electors.

An election for the office of president of the United States is an exciting, expensive, and long affair. The process begins with the selection of candidates by political parties. Before the national parties select their candidates, the state parties decide whom to support at the national party conventions.

By their own choice, 31 states hold primary (practice) elections to show which of the two parties' candidates are the most popular with their voters. Delegates to each party's national convention generally support the candidate who won their state primary.

After the primaries are over, the parties hold their conventions. These are usually like colorful, noisy, and enthusiastic parties. Political parties in each state choose the delegates who will attend that party's convention. States have different rules for delegate selection.

Once at the convention, supporters wave signs and banners for their candidate, and listen to speeches by party leaders.

Meanwhile, the candidates work frantically to be sure they have the delegates they need when the actual balloting (voting) begins. As the name of each state is called, the head of the delegation announces the delegates' vote for a particular candidate. Often the final candidate is selected on the first ballot, but sometimes many ballots are needed. The party's final candidate must then select a vice-president and present this running mate to the convention.

Once the conventions are over, the second and hardest part of the presidential election begins. The candidates of each party set out to convince the American voters of their qualifications.

Today the Electoral College works differently. Before a presidential election, each political party in each state selects its electors. When voters go to the polls and vote for their choice of candidates, they are actually voting for electors from each candidate's party. In most states the electors' names don't even appear on the ballot.

When the popular vote has been counted, the electors of the winning party are declared to be the state's official electors. In December, the electors from each state go to their state capitals and cast their votes. The votes are sent to the Senate, where they are counted.

The formal counting of the electoral votes takes place in the Senate on January 6. The president of the Senate counts the votes before an audience of the members of both houses of Congress. The candidates with the majority of the electoral votes for the offices of president and vice-president are declared the winners.

If no candidate has a majority, the House of Representatives elects the president from the candidates (no more than three) with the most votes, and the Senate elects the vice-president in the same way from the two candidates with the most votes. When the House elects the president, each state has one vote.

Three times in history the candidate with the greatest number of popular votes nationwide did not receive the majority of the electoral votes—and did not become president. This can happen because all of a state's electoral votes must go to the candidate with the majority of the popular vote in that state. For example, in 1888, Grover Cleveland received the most popular votes in more states across the country than Benjamin Harrison (served 1889–1893). But Cleveland's states were the smaller ones that had fewer electoral votes. In the more heavily populated states, which have more electoral votes, Cleveland had almost as many popular votes as Harrison, which added to his popular votes overall. But since Harrison won the majority of the votes in the big states, he earned all of their electoral votes. Therefore, Harrison was finally elected president because he had more *electoral* votes.

Most people agree that the Electoral College system is too clumsy. It legally carries out the instructions of the Constitution, but it certainly does not work the way the Founders intended. However, the system is very hard to replace. Over the years, there have been many suggestions for ways to change the electoral system, but none of them was supported by both individual voters and the states.

Even though the election process is long and complicated, it is meant to ensure that America's leader is chosen fairly. Because the president is a chief symbol of our nation and a powerful head of government, Americans must believe that their president will serve their country in a way that protects the interests and freedoms of all our citizens. **45**

Glossary

bill   A proposed law.

delegate   A person authorized to represent others.

economy   The management of the income and expenses of a government; plus the nation's production and consumption of goods and services.

electoral vote   Presidential and vice-presidential votes cast by members of the Electoral College, representing the population of the states.

executive   The part of the government that has the power to carry out duties and functions necessary to enforce the laws.

habeas corpus   A writ (legal document) that prevents people from being arrested without evidence against them.

impeach   To try a public official on charges of wrongdoing.

judiciary   The part of the government that administers justice.

legislative   The part of the government with the power to make laws.

primary   A preliminary election in which candidates are chosen for the final election.

pro tempore   Temporary, as in acting in someone else's absence.

veto   The power of a president to reject a bill passed by Congress.

For Further Reading

Beard, Charles A. *The Presidents in American History.* New York: Julian Messner, 1991.

Green, C., and Sanford, W. *The Presidency.* Vero Beach: Rourke, 1990.

Greene, C. *Presidents.* Chicago: Childrens Press, 1989.

Johnson, Linda Carlson. *The Constitution.* Brookfield: The Millbrook Press, 1992.

Kent, Zachary. *Franklin D. Roosevelt.* Chicago: Childrens Press, 1989.

McPhillips, Martin. *The Constitutional Convention.* Morristown: Silver Burdett Press, 1985.

Schlesinger, Arthur M., Jr., ed. *The Presidency.* Broomall: Chelsea House, 1990.

Index